Understanding NFS

Sujata Biswas

Content

Introduction

This is a quick guide to getting up and ready with NFS on Centos and Ubuntu.

Prerequisites

You must have some knowledge of any Linux Operating System and Networking.

Chapter 1: What is NFS?

TCP Primer

TCP/IP is a crucial communication protocol that provides a set of rules for transferring data between devices on a network. It is not just a framework, but a complete suite of protocols that work together to ensure that data is transmitted reliably and efficiently.

In order for communication to take place between two devices on a network, they must both adhere to the same set of rules. This is where TCP/IP comes in - it provides a common language that allows devices to communicate with each other effectively. It specifies how data packets should be transmitted, how they should be formatted, and how errors should be handled.

Back in the day, there were other communication protocols such as IPX/SPX, which were used by some networks. However, these protocols have become obsolete, and TCP/IP has emerged as the standard protocol for most modern networks. This is because TCP/IP is an open protocol, meaning it is not proprietary, and it has been widely adopted by different vendors.

TCP/IP is often associated with other protocols that work together to provide different network services. For instance, FTP (File Transfer Protocol) and NFS (Network File System) use TCP/IP to transfer files between devices on a network. HTTP (Hypertext Transfer Protocol), which is used to transfer data over the World Wide Web, also relies on TCP/IP.

In conclusion, TCP/IP is a vital protocol that enables communication between devices on a network. It provides a common language that allows different devices and protocols to work together effectively. As the backbone of the internet and other modern networks, TCP/IP has become an essential part of our daily lives.

NFS Primer

NFS, or Network File System, is a protocol designed by Sun Microsystems for sharing files over a network. It is implemented by various vendors and has become a popular method for sharing directories and files among systems.

The NFS protocol allows a system to share its directories on the network, which can be mounted across other systems running the client version of NFS implementation. The system that shares its directories must run the server-level implementation of NFS. Once the directories of the NFS server are mounted on the client system(s), they act as if they are part of the local hierarchy. This makes it easy for users to access files on remote systems as if they were stored locally.

One of the most significant advantages of NFS is its ability to create a distributed file system across multiple systems. This allows for efficient sharing of resources and can save a significant amount of time and effort when managing large networks. For example, when you install production-ready software on a server running the NFS server daemons and make it available to the client nodes to mount, many clients can access the software that you have installed on one machine. This eliminates the need to install the software on each client system, saving valuable time and resources.

However, there are some downsides to using NFS. If the server machine fails, all clients may become useless, creating a single point of failure. This issue can be alleviated by using RAID, or Redundant Array of Inexpensive Disks, to ensure redundancy and protect against data loss. Additionally, NFS may lead to a situation where it appears that there is not enough work to do. As a result, it is important to be judicious in deciding what resources to share and to carefully monitor network usage to ensure optimal performance.

In summary, NFS is a powerful and flexible protocol that facilitates the sharing of hierarchies across the network. While it has some limitations, it remains a popular choice for organizations seeking to streamline network management and improve collaboration among users.

NFS Theory

NFS is not a standalone protocol, it closely associated with TCP/IP and uses a range of protocols to service its client-server architecture. To understand the concepts, we must refer to the OSI Model. The International Organization of Standards (OSI) developed this landmark model in 1978 with the aim of using it as a basis to create open systems, and that different architecture should adhere to a common set of rules for communication. Because during those tumultuous early periods, vendors created a proprietary architecture. The real reason, which, of course, is my opinion, is that the vendors used such tactics to give less choice to customers and protect their businesses. However, adherence to OSI model ultimately proved beneficial paving the way for heterogenous architecture and allowing interoperability.

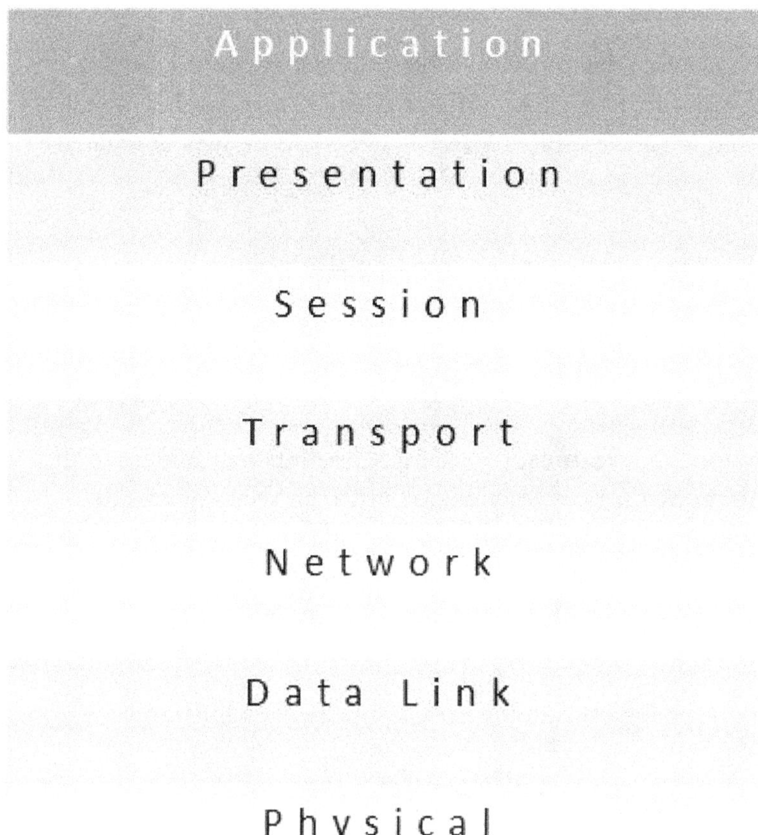

Open System Interconnections Model

As you can see, the OSI has 7 layers. The top layer is the application layer and corresponds to applications/protocols such as FTP, NFS, the now-dreaded TELNET, HTTP. Consider a grain of sand, that needs to traverse from the Physical Layer and to the Application Layer, as it crosses each layer, imagine a coat of paint added to it at every layer until it becomes a pearl when it reaches the top layer. The grain of sand is of course an analogy for the bit of data. In a reversal, when the pearl travels down, each coating is stripped off, until it becomes the lonesome single grain of sand (a bit) again.

Note: The TELNET is unpopular because it sends passwords without encryption, creating a security problem. I think telnet is a nice tool to check TCP/IP connectivity between two nodes and also for determining close or open TCP ports.

Let's understand how NFS maps to each layer of the OSI Model with a brief description of their functions:

Physical Layer:

As the name suggests, it deals with the hardware that includes cables, the network card, wireless/wired network. The layer deal with bits in the form of **Zeros** and **Ones** – called digital communication. The layer is not bothered what these bits represent - it could be files or database records or ping echoes.

As for NFS, it supports all the underlying hardware components of the Physical layer.

Data Link Layer:

The bits from the Physical layer are grouped into **frames**, for example, the bits may adhere to the Ethernet protocol frame format. The frame is a sort of an envelope in which your data resides. Moreover, like a real envelope, the frame consists of Address, control, data and error-control fields. For example, the address field has both the source and destination address for the data it is carrying. The main function of this layer is to pass the frames to the next layer – Network.

As with Physical layer, NFS also supports the logical framing services of the data link layer.

Network layer:

The evolution of technology has brought about changes in the networking world as well. One such change is the renaming of frames in the Data Link Layer to packets in the Network Layer. The Network Layer, which facilitates routing of packets between nodes, also allows for connectivity between different types of networks. This is achieved through a set of rules provided by the Network Layer, which acts as a common ground between the two networks. This set of rules is based on addressing, like the Data Link Layer, where an envelope contains the source and destination addresses.

In addition, the Network Layer is associated with IP packets, as it is these packets that carry data and are reassembled at the destination. The beauty of the Network Layer is that it is more than happy to use IP packets, allowing for seamless communication across networks. This is where NFS comes into play. Developed by Sun Microsystems and implemented by many vendors, NFS is a distributed file system protocol that enables sharing of hierarchies across the network.

A practical use case of NFS is installing a production-ready software on a server running the NFS server daemons, making it available to client nodes to mount. This allows many clients to access the software installed on a single machine, saving valuable time that would have been spent installing the software on each client system. However, there are downsides to NFS, such as a single point of failure if the server machine fails, and the risk of being seen as having not enough work to do. Thus, judicious usage is necessary to ensure optimal performance.

Transport layer:

This layer is all about data integrity and error control mechanism. It can be considered as an extension of the Network Layer but with more emphasis on error control. If the previous layers have failed to provide better error control to the packets, it falls upon the Transport Layer to provide the necessary services to compensate the lack. The two protocols associated with Transport Layer are UDP (User Datagram Protocol) and TCP.

Earlier versions of NFS used UDP, like version 1 and version 2. However, even later revisions of NFS 2 started to support TCP. While UDP is fast, it is not reliable. TCP is slow because it added error control mechanisms to the packets. UDP is faster because it does not employ error control and sends no acknowledgment of data delivery. TCP is bogged down by error controls and sends an acknowledgment to the sender.

Session Layer:

As the name suggests, a link or a session is established between two nodes in this layer. The layer provides a mechanism for dialog control between two communicating nodes. For example, if you are downloading a file from a remote system and the connection terminates due to a network outage, a control mechanism called "synchronization check point" is built-in in the packets is referred to; so that when network connectivity is restored, you can start downloading from the point it lost the communication.

A protocol that provides more services than the regular TCP/IP and is used by NFS extensively is the RPC or Remote Procedure Call. However, many other applications/protocols do not need to adhere to the standards dictated by this layer. RPC is a set of libraries that provide an abstraction layer from the lower OSI layers while giving access to NFS to higher levels such as Presentation and Application layers.

Remote Procedure Calls are implemented by NFS; these are specialized programs that deal with the transfer of data and control commands. Initially, these commands were used in applications on a single computer, for instance copying a file from one directory to another. Over time, the folks at Xerox thought that they could be implemented over the network as well. If you want to know more about RPC, then google for RFC (Request for Comments) number 1831.

Presentation Layer:

This is the layer that concerns how the data presented to you looks. NFS uses the XDR (External Data Representation) protocol in this layer.

Application Layer:

Application Programming Protocols (APIs) form the basis of this layer; there are libraries that developers use to create network applications. The services provided by this layer are followed by most of the applications like NFS, HTTP, FTP).

The Services are:

- Providing libraries that enable read and write into remote hierarchies.
- Executing commands on remote locations.
- Enabling messaging between nodes.

Chapter 2: Pre-Installation Activities and Installation of NFS server and client

Documentation

The first step is documentation of hostname, designation of server and client roles, a collection of IP addresses.

Hostname	**IP address**	**Role**	**Operating System**
centos7	192.168.1.5	Server	Centos 7
Ubuntu1604	192.168.1.12	Client	Ubuntu 16.04

Installation of NFS server on Centos

Step 1

You need to install the packages on the NFS server. The packages are:

- **nfs-utils**
- **rpcbind**

Login as root and enter the following commands:

 # yum install nfs-utils

 # yum install rpcbind

To know about the packages that you have installed, run the **rpm** command **-qi** options and read the description.

 # rpm -qi rpcbind-0.2.0-42.el7.x86_64

The description says:

Description:

The rpcbind utility is a server that converts RPC program numbers into universal addresses. It must be running on the host to be able to make RPC calls on a server on that machine.

Source: "Description" is the Output of the **rpm -qi** *command from Centos Machine*

 # rpm -qi nfs-utils.x86_64

Description:

The nfs-utils package provides a daemon for the kernel NFS server and related tools, which provides a much higher level of performance than the traditional Linux NFS server used by most users.

This package also contains the showmount program. Showmount queries the mount daemon on a remote host for information about the NFS (Network File System) server on the remote host. For example, showmount can display the clients which are mounted on that host.

This package also contains the mount.nfs and umount.nfs program.

Source: "Description" is the Output of the **rpm -qi** *command from Centos Machine*

Step 2

Create a directory on the Centos machine that you wish to share.

 # mkdir centos7_share

Go to the directory and create 10 empty files with touch and the following construct.

 # touch abc{1..10}

The **etc** directory is the repository of configuration files used by many TCP/IP applications; you need to update a file called **exports** and enter the name of the directory you wish to share across the network. In this case, the directory is **centos7_share**, followed by the permissions in brackets.

 # cat exports
/centos7_share (rw)

The **rw** indicates Read and Write permissions for all the Servers on the network.

Now, give all permissions to the **/centos7_share** directory:

drwxrwxrwx. 2 root root 127 Dec 9 22:04 centos7_share

<u>Step 3</u>

Create the same set of users on both the server and the client. The users will have to have the same names and UID (User Identifier). You can see the UIDs in **/etc/passwd** file.

 # useradd -u 2017 -m nfslogin1

 # useradd -u 2018 -m nfslogin2

Using the **passwd** command to change the password. Keep it same.

Now, **ssh** to the Ubuntu server and create the two same users:

$ sudo useradd -u 2017 -m nfslogin1

$ sudo useradd -u 2017 -m nfslogin1

Using the **passwd** command to change the password. Keep it same.

Note:

While trying to **ssh** to the Ubuntu server, you may get the following message:

 # ssh 192.168.1.12
ssh: connect to host 192.168.1.12 port 22: Connection refused

You need to install the **openssh** package and start the **ssh** service on Ubuntu

$ sudo apt-get install openssh-server

$ sudo systemctl restart ssh

When you **ssh** to Ubuntu, remember that there is no root user, so you must login to Centos with another user.

<u>Step 4</u>

Starting the NFS related services on Centos:

 # service nfs start
Redirecting to /bin/systemctl start nfs.service

 # service rpcbind start
Redirecting to /bin/systemctl start rpcbind.service

To verify if the folder is shared **(/centos7_share**), enter the following command:

 # exportfs
/centos7_share <world>

Moreover, so, it is verified.

Step 5

The client installation on Ubuntu is relatively simple

$ sudo apt-get install nfs-common

Create a directory inside **/mnt**

$ sudo mkdir share_centos7

Mount the shared file system from the Centos7 server on Ubuntu:

$ sudo mount 192.168.1.5:/centos7_share /mnt/share_centos7

```
$ ls -l /mnt/share_centos7
    total 0
-rw-r--r-- 1 root root 0 Dec  9 22:04 abc1
-rw-r--r-- 1 root root 0 Dec  9 22:04 abc10
-rw-r--r-- 1 root root 0 Dec  9 22:04 abc2
-rw-r--r-- 1 root root 0 Dec  9 22:04 abc3
-rw-r--r-- 1 root root 0 Dec  9 22:04 abc4
-rw-r--r-- 1 root root 0 Dec  9 22:04 abc5
-rw-r--r-- 1 root root 0 Dec  9 22:04 abc6
-rw-r--r-- 1 root root 0 Dec  9 22:04 abc7
-rw-r--r-- 1 root root 0 Dec  9 22:04 abc8
-rw-r--r-- 1 root root 0 Dec  9 22:04 abc9
```

Staying on Ubuntu, login as **nfslogin1** and create a file and then go back to Centos NFS server and check what you see.

$ su nfslogin1

```
$ ls -l hello_from_Ubuntu
-rw-rw-r-- 1 nfslogin1 nfslogin1 0 Dec  9 23:16 hello_from_Ubuntu
```

We go back to Centos and see the ownership and group of the file **hello_from_Ubuntu**

$ ls -l hello_from_Ubuntu
-rw-rw-r--. 1 nfslogin1 nfslogin1 0 Dec 9 23:16 hello_from_Ubuntu

There we have it. The basic NFS Server – Client configuration across two different Operating systems.

However, why a same set of users is created on the Server and the Client?

In the case of NFS, the set of users created on the server and the client are necessary to ensure that the client machine can access the shared directories on the server machine with the correct permissions. When a server shares its directories on the network, it sets permissions for different users or groups that determine who can read, write, or execute files in those directories.

To access these directories, the client machine needs to have the same set of users and groups as the server, so that the client can be mapped to the appropriate user or group on the server that has the necessary permissions to access the shared directories. This mapping is done using a process called user and group mapping, where the client machine maps its local users and groups to the corresponding users and groups on the server.

Without this mapping, the client machine may not have the necessary permissions to access the shared directories and may be denied access or only granted limited access. So, it is important to ensure that the same set of users and groups are created on both the server and client machines, and that they are mapped correctly, to enable seamless access to shared directories on the network.

Chapter 3 Advanced NFS configuration

Setting up an Ubuntu Server-Client NFS configuration with advanced options

Step 1

As always documentation is the first step, in this example, we will use the following systems:

Hostname	IP address	Role	Operating System
bobby-vm	192.168.1.8	Server	Ubuntu 17.04
sujata-vm	192.168.1.7	Client	Ubuntu 16.04.3

Step 2

Make sure that both client and server's **/etc/hosts** have their own and each other's IP address to hostname mapping for local resolution.

Both the **hosts** file, for this example, must have the following entries:

192.168.1.8 bobby-vm
192.168.1.7 sujata-vm

To test, if the settings are working, ping with the hostnames

$ ping bobby-vm
PING bobby-vm (192.168.1.8) 56(84) bytes of data.
64 bytes from bobby-vm (192.168.1.8): icmp_seq=1 ttl=64 time=0.576 ms

$ ping sujata-vm
PING sujata-vm (192.168.1.7) 56(84) bytes of data.
64 bytes from sujata-vm (192.168.1.7): icmp_seq=1 ttl=64 time=0.415 ms

Step 3

Login to the server**, bobby-vm**, to install the utilities for the NFS server using the yum command:

$ sudo apt-get install nfs-kernel-server rpcbind nfs-common

Refer to the following table about the information on each package that has been installed:

Package Name	**DESCRIPTION**
nfs-kernel-server	The NFS kernel server is currently the recommended NFS server for use with Linux, featuring features such as NFSv3 and NFSv4, Kerberos support via GSS, and much more. It is also significantly faster and usually more reliable than the user-space NFS servers (from the unfs3 and nfs-user-server packages). However, it is more difficult to debug than the user-space servers and has a slightly different feature set. This package contains the user-space support needed to use the NFS kernel server. **Most administrators wishing to set up an NFS server would want to install this package.**
rpcbind	Converts RPC program numbers into universal addresses. The rpcbind utility is a server that converts RPC program numbers into universal addresses
nfs-common	NFS support files common to client and server Use this package on any machine that uses NFS, either as client or server. Programs included: lockd, statd, showmount, nfsstat, gssd, idmapd and mount.nfs.

Source: The DESCRIPTION is sourced from the output of the command **$ sudo apt-cache show <package_name>**

Step 4

Create two directories on the NFS server, **bobby-vm**, to be shared.

$ sudo mkdir /share1
$ sudo mkdir /share2

Since the directories were created using **sudo**, the owner and the group to which it belongs to is **the root**:

$ ls -l

drwxr-xr-x 2 root root 4096 Dec 10 17:24 share1
drwxr-xr-x 2 root root 4096 Dec 10 17:25 share2

NFS does not allow **root** to perform any operations, so you must change the ownership of the directory to "**nobody**" and the group to "**nogroup**"

$ sudo chown nobody share1 share2

$ sudo chgrp nogroup share1 share2

drwxr-xr-x 2 nobody nogroup 4096 Dec 10 17:24 share1
drwxr-xr-x 2 nobody nogroup 4096 Dec 10 17:25 share2

Go to each directory and create some files. Even if you create some files, the ownership and group will still be **root**. You must make changes again with **chown** and **chgrp** commands.

Step 5

Exporting the directories to the network, for this we need to access the **/etc/exports** file. The syntax of putting entries is as follows:

directory <client(s)>(permissions, sync_operations, no-subtree-check, no-root-squash)

Note: You should look at **man exports** page for more exhaustive options.

The following table explains the commonest options of the exports file syntax.

Options	Descriptions
client(s)	Is hostname of the clients(s). You can put the IP Address and FQDN (Fully Qualified Domain Name). It even supports * so that all clients can mount the exported directory.
permissions	Commonly, **ro** (read-only) or **rw** (read and write) permissions are used. When you give **ro**, the client can mount the directory in Read Only mode.
sync_operations	If the client performs a write operation on a file that exists in the exported directory, this option forces the change to sync with a hard disk of the NFS server.
no-subtree-check	This option inactivates sub-tree checking, means that NFS does not know if the file in the exported directory exists there or is like any other file in the file system. If this is not set to **no**, then for every client operation on file in the exported directory, NFS will try to check if the file exists and may slow down access to files from a remote system. Thus, it is always recommended to disable the option.
no_root_squash	In a production environment, it is imperative that you disable this option with **no_root_squash**. Otherwise, the root user at the client will have the same privileges as the root user of the NFS server.

Open the **exports** file in **/etc** in the server and put the following directories with different options.

$ tail -2 exports

/share1 sujata-vm(rw,sync,no_subtree_check)
/share2 sujata-vm(ro,sync,no_root_squash)

Start the process with the following command:

$ sudo systemctl restart nfs-kernel-
server $
Use the following command to see if our configuration has been successful or not.

$ sudo exportfs

/share1 sujata-vm
/share2 sujata-vm

It sure looks good for now. Let's configure the client.

There is another command you run to check the status of the exported directories:

$ showmount -e

Export list for bobby-vm:

/share2 sujata-vm
/share1 sujata-vm

Step 6

Install the NFS client software on the client:

$ sudo apt-get install nfs-common

Step 7

Create mount points on the client.

$ cd /mnt

$ sudo mkdir bobby1
$ sudo mkdir bobby2

Mounts points on the client system, **sujata-vm**, are **bobby1** and **bobby2.**

Step 8

Mounting remote directories on the client machine. The syntaxes are as follows:

sudo mount IP_ADDR_NFS_SERVER:/nfs_server_shared_dir /client_mount_dir

sudo mount HOSTNAME: /nfs_server_shared_dir /client_mount_dir

Example 1:

sudo mount 192.168.1.8:/share1 /mnt/bobby1

Example 2:

sudo mount bobby-vm:/share2 /mnt/bobby2

Let's create a file in **/mnt/bobby1** (client) and check if the file is visible on the server **bobby-vm**.

$ sudo touch hello_from_sujata

$ ls -l
total 0
-rw-r--r-- 1 nobody nogroup 0 Dec 10 22:05 hello_from_sujata

As you can see the ownership and group of the new file are correct. Though we created the file as **sudo** on the client, the ownership and group is not root. The root cannot perform administrative tasks on this NFS mounted the drive. Look what happens, when as root you try to change the ownership of the file that we just created:

$ sudo chown root *
chown: changing ownership of 'hello_from_sujata': Operation not permitted

Let's see if the file is visible on the NFS server **/share1** directory:

```
bobby@bobby-vm:/share1$ ls -l
total 0
-rw-r--r-- 1 nobody nogroup 0 Dec 10 22:05 hello_from_sujata
bobby@bobby-vm:/share1$ hostname
bobby-vm
```

Snapshot from the server, bobby-vm.

Yes, it is visible.

Checking the size of the mounted directories

You use the normal **df -k** command on the client to check the disk status. It can also give you a clue if the shared directory is mounted or not. Many unpleasant surprises in life.

```
$ df -h

Filesystem          Size  Used Avail Use% Mounted on

udev               474M     0  474M   0% /dev tmpfs
100M  3.6M   96M   4% /run /dev/sda1           14G
3.9G  9.0G  31% / tmpfs                 496M  136K  495M
1% /dev/shm tmpfs               5.0M  4.0K  5.0M   1%
/run/lock tmpfs              496M     0  496M   0%
/sys/fs/cgroup tmpfs             100M   48K   99M
1% /run/user/1000 192.168.1.8:/share1  11G  4.5G
5.8G  44% /mnt/bobby1 bobby-vm:/share2      11G
4.5G  5.8G  44% /mnt/bobby2
```

Unmounting a shared directory

The **umount** command is used to unmount the shared directory.

```
$ sudo umount /mnt/bobby2
[sudo] password for sujata:
```

```
$ df -h
Filesystem          Size  Used Avail Use% Mounted on
    .
    .
    .
tmpfs               100M   48K   99M   1% /run/user/1000
192.168.1.8:/share1   11G  4.5G  5.8G  44% /mnt/bobby1
```

We can see from **df -h**, that **/mnt/bobby2** has been successfully unmounted.

Boot time mounting of the remote NFS directory.

To enable boot-time mounting of NFS mounts, you must configure the **fstab** file in **/etc** directory.

$ sudo nano /etc/fstab

Add the entry: **bobby-vm:/share2**

/mnt/bobby2 nfs4 rw 0 0

The last fields, 0, 0 are for Ubuntu not to run file system disk-checking executable during boot time. You need to reboot **sujata-vm** and check the **df -h** command.

Now, to check the **df -h** command:

```
sujata@sujata-vm:~$ df -h
Filesystem         Size  Used Avail Use% Mounted on
udev               474M     0  474M   0% /dev
tmpfs              100M  3.6M   96M   4% /run
/dev/sda1           14G  3.9G  9.0G  31% /
tmpfs              496M  172K  495M   1% /dev/shm
tmpfs              5.0M  4.0K  5.0M   1% /run/lock
tmpfs              496M     0  496M   0% /sys/fs/cgroup
bobby-vm:/share2    11G  4.5G  5.8G  44% /mnt/bobby2
tmpfs              100M   52K   99M   1% /run/user/1000
```

We can see that boot-time mounting is successful.

Note:

Do not even think of trying such activities on a production server, a mistake can bring the Ubuntu to an Administrative mode, if lucky. Alternatively, worse, if unlucky – which is more common. Your Boss will remember this mistake, like, forever.

Chapter: 5 Troubleshooting NFS

Why do I get the "device is busy" error when I try to unmount a directory on the client?

When I try to unmount a shared directory, I get the following error:

$ sudo umount /mnt/bobby1

[sudo] password for sujata:

umount.nfs4: /mnt/bobby1: device is busy

The most likely reason is that someone has opened a file residing in **/mnt/bobby1**, to check if that is the case, execute the **lsof** (list of open files) command:

$ sudo lsof /mnt/bobby1

lsof: WARNING: can't stat() fuse.gvfsd-fuse file system /run/user/1000/gvfs Output information may be incomplete.

COMMAND PID USER FD TYPE DEVICE SIZE/OFF NODE NAME
bash 1478 sujata cwd DIR 0,43 4096 262166 /mnt/bobby1 (192.168.1.8:/share1) sudo 1528 root cwd DIR 0,43 4096 262166 /mnt/bobby1 (192.168.1.8:/share1) nano 1530 root cwd DIR 0,43 4096 262166 /mnt/bobby1 (192.168.1.8:/share1)

It is indeed, a bit hard to make out what is happening, but the last entry is giving a clue of sorts, that someone (root, in this case) is using **nano** (the editor).

In some cases, you have to ask the user to log out, because even closing the application at her/his end may not resolve the issue of the device is a busy error.

When I try to umount on the client, I get the error "umount failed: Operation not permitted"?

You get this error when you do not use sudo:

$ umount /mnt/bobby1

umount: /mnt/bobby1: umount failed: Operation not permitted

Using **sudo** resolves the problem.

I have weird problems while trying to mount directories on the client, why do I get a process hang?

Error:

I get a hang when I try to mount a directory.

sujata@sujata-vm:~$ sudo mount /mnt/bobby2

<Nothing Happens>

The issue could be related to firewall settings. Check the status of the firewall on the **NFS server** using the following command:

$ sudo ufw status

```
bobby@bobby-vm:/share1$ sudo  ufw status
Status: active

To                          Action      From
--                          ------      ----
2049                        DENY        192.168.1.7
```

While no one will explicitly set the rule (unless he/she is your office enemy – and such characters do exist). However, it is always safer to check the firewall for weird problems. So, what is the number 2049, it is the PORT used by NFS to listen to client requests? The quickest action you can perform is to disable the firewall to narrow down the issue. Again, you must be very careful if it were a production server.

The command to disable the firewall is:

$ sudo disable ufw

```
bobby@bobby-vm:~$ sudo ufw disable
[sudo] password for bobby:
Firewall stopped and disabled on system startup
```

However, disabling firewall is fine while testing, but you must get the firewall up and running again otherwise you may be violating your security policy which may have legal implication depending in the industry you are in.

To delete the rule, following the steps:

$ sudo ufw status numbered

Status: active

To	Action	From
--	------	----
[1] 2049	DENY	IN 192.168.1.7

To delete the rule, enter:

$ sudo ufw delete 1

Deleting: deny from 192.168.1.7
to any port 2049
Proceed with operation (y|n)? y
Rule deleted

Check status again:

$ sudo ufw status
Status: active

As we can see from the status no rule is defined. Let's use define rules for the port used by NFS 2049, additionally, also define port 111. This is the port that is used by RPC, some implementation of NFS may use this port as well.

You can get a list of ports used by various daemons, by looking at the content of the **/etc/services** file.

$ cat /etc/services | grep 111 sunrpc 111/tcp
portmapper # RPC 4.0 portmapper sunrpc
111/udp portmapper

Note: Sun Microsystems was one of the first companies to implement NFS, hence the name sunrpc.

$ cat /etc/services | grep 2049
nfs 2049/tcp # Network File
System nfs 2049/udp # Network
File System

Now, define the ports (perform this activity on the System Console):

$ sudo ufw allow 22
Rule added
Rule Added (v6)
Note: Port 22 is the port for SSH.

$ sudo ufw allow 2049/tcp
Rule added
Rule Added (v6)

$ sudo ufw allow 2049/udp
Rule added
Rule Added (v6)

$ sudo ufw allow 111/tcp
Rule added
Rule Added (v6)

$ sudo ufw allow 111/udp
Rule added
Rule Added (v6)

Let's check the status of the firewall:

$ sudo ufw status
Status: active

To Action From

```
--                    ------  ----
22                    ALLOW   Anywhere
    2049/tcp          ALLOW   Anywhere
    2049/udp          ALLOW   Anywhere
    111/udp           ALLOW   Anywhere
    111/tcp           ALLOW   Anywhere
    22 (v6)           ALLOW   Anywhere (v6)
    2049/tcp (v6)     ALLOW   Anywhere (v6)
    2049/udp (v6)     ALLOW   Anywhere (v6)
    111/udp (v6)      ALLOW   Anywhere (v6)
    111/tcp (v6)      ALLOW   Anywhere (v6)
```

Which Commands should I use for troubleshooting NFS issues?

Apart from checking connectivity using the **ping** command, you can use the **telnet** command to troubleshoot as well. We all know that the "modern" system administrators frown upon using **telnet** due to its unsafe nature. However, personally, I use it to troubleshoot. However, the process to install telnet is hazardous and frustrating.

Here's a method how to install and configure **telnet** on Ubuntu:

Step 1 : Install the package:

sudo apt-get install xinetd telnetd

Step 2: Check with **which** command if its installed:

$ which telnet
/usr/bin/telnet

However, when you **telnet** your loopback address or any other address for that matter, you get connection refused error. Create a file called **inetd.conf**

Note: Before making any changes in configuration files in **/etc** make a copy of that file (if the file exists).

$ sudo nano /etc/inetd.conf

And add the following entry:

telnet stream tcp nowait telnetd /usr/sbin/tcpd /usr/sbin/in.telnetd

Save and exit.

sudo /etc/init.d/xinetd restart

Note: Many old utilities are clubbed together inside the **xinetd** daemon. When I was starting out, we studied this daemon very carefully.

Now, **telnet** should work.

You can use telnet for the following activities:

1) Right after using **ping** to check connectivity. Telnet your loopback address and the remote server to ensure that TCP/IP connectivity is perfect. Remember, ping sends ICMP (Internet Control Message Protocol) packets.
2) To check if the NFS port 2049 is functioning properly, we can at least find out if the port is blocked by the firewall or now.

When we **telnet** from the client, **sujata-vm**, to the remote system, **bobby-vm**, we get the correct output, asking for login credentials:

$ telnet 192.168.1.8
Trying 192.168.1.8...
Connected to 192.168.1.8.
Escape character is
'^]'. Ubuntu 17.04
bobby-vm login:

However, when we use the port used by NFS 2049, we get the following message, you do not see the program asking for login, indicating that the port is used by some other service.

$ telnet 192.168.1.8 2049
Trying 192.168.1.8...
Connected to 192.168.1.8.

```
Escape character is '^]'.
```

Now, let's see the impact if we shut down the NFS service on the server.

$ sudo systemctl stop nfs-kernel-server #This Action takes place on the NFS server

Obviously, NFS is no longer "listening" for client connection, and the port is free (on the server), you can check by using **telnet** from the client. See what you get.

```
telnet 192.168.1.8 2049
Trying 192.168.1.8...
telnet: Unable to connect to remote host: Connection refused
```

No service is using the port, and hence the connection has been refused. However, if you telnet using the port 23 that is used by **telnet** and it is in the listening mode, you will get a successful login as shown below:

```
$ telnet 192.168.1.8 23
Trying 192.168.1.8...
Connected to 192.168.1.8.
Escape character is
'^]'. Ubuntu 17.04
bobby-vm login:
```

Note: Be sure to add the rule **sudo ufw allow 23/tcp** , if your firewall is enabled.

Another command that you can use from client is **nfsstat**, particularly if the user is complaining about slowness, the **-c** option is client.

```
$ sudo nfsstat -c

Client rpc stats: calls
retrans    authrefrsh
360     0       360

Client nfs v4:
```

```
null       read       write      commit     open
open_conf 0        0% 0       0% 0       0% 0       0% 38
10% 1      0% open_noat   open_dgrd   close
setattr    fsinfo     renew 0        0% 0       0% 1
0% 1       0% 6       1% 212     60% setclntid    confirm
lock       lockt      locku      access 17     4% 4
1% 0       0% 0       0% 0       0% 10      2% getattr
lookup     lookup_root remove      rename     link 26
7% 16      4% 2       0% 0       0% 0       0% 0       0%
symlink    create     pathconf    statfs     readlink
readdir 0      0% 0       0% 4       1% 1       0% 0
0% 4       1%
server_caps delegreturn getacl      setacl     fs_locations rel_lkowner
10      2% 0       0% 0       0% 0       0% 0       0% 0       0%
secinfo    exchange_id create_ses  destroy_ses sequence    get_lease_t
0       0% 0       0% 0       0% 0       0% 0       0% 0       0%
reclaim_comp layoutget   getdevinfo  layoutcommit layoutreturn getdevlist
0       0% 0       0% 0       0% 0       0% 0       0% 0
0% (null)
0       0%
```

Look at the field called "retrans" (retransmission), if the number of restrans is a certain percentage of the total number of "calls", then you may have to dig further. What you need to do is subjective to your environment, a snapshot of normal activity should be compared when things go wrong.

You can also explore the **showmount** command – which we studied earlier. The man page for **showmount** in Ubuntu looks good – though it seems it was written in 1993.

$ sudo showmount -e

Export list for bobby-vm:
/share2 sujata-vm
/share1 sujata-vm

How do I implement AutoFS ?

Autofs is an implementation of NFS that saves network bandwidth because it is only enabled when a user accesses it and then automatically times out the shared directories when it is not being used.

Pre-installation activities:

- In this example, the same systems will be used, **bobby-vm** and **sujata-vm**.

Actions on sujata-vm (the NFS client) to prepare for the autonfs preparation

- Umount the shared directories
- Comment out the automatic loading of mounted directories from **/etc/fastab** file. Don't destroy the entries though.

Actions on bobby-vm (the NFS server)

- You should do nothing here beyond ensuring that the NFS server is still running

$ sudo exportfs
/share1 sujata-vm
/share2 sujata-vm

Installation of autofs package on the client sujata-vm:

You will install the following package on Ubuntu

$ sudo apt-get install autofs

While installing **autofs**, several configuration files are copied in the **/etc** directory.

Autofs configuration files:

Configuration file	Description

/etc/auto.master	This is the master configuration file. It is also called the Master Map. The contents of the file are names of the **autofs** mapped points with a wrapper map file location, followed by options, such as: **#/misc /etc/auto.misc**
Map files	Consider /**misc /etc/auto.misc** - this entry tells **autofs** to look at the map file **auto.misc** and make mount-points in **/misc** directory as per auto.misc. Such a map is called indirect map. There are direct maps as well, autofs should refer to the **auto.map** file to know where to create the mount points. In the previous example, the direction to autofs is indirect. The direct map entry looks like: **./ /etc/auto.data** Remember, each mount in **autofs** has its own map file.

Step 1:

Create a mount point in the master file, **auto.master**

Entering the following in **auto.master**:

/new /etc/auto.nfs

Where **new is the mount point,** and **auto.nfs** is its map file. Remember **new** is the MOUNT point.

Step 2:

Creation of auto.nfs file with the following entries

$ cat /etc/auto.nfs

share1 -fstype=nfs4 192.168.1.8:/share1
share2 -fstype=nfs4 192.168.1.8:/share2

Where:

Keys	File System type	IP address : / share_directory
share1	nfs4	192.168.1.8:/share1 IP ADDRESS of **bobby-vm**
share2	nfs4	192.168.1.8:/share2 IP ADDRESS of **bobby-vm**

Each share will have its own line. These entries are relative to the entries in **auto.master** file, the mounts will be **/new/<shared_directory>** on the client. Since the NFS implementation is version 4, you should explicitly state that in the **auto.nfs** file (File System Type = nfs4).

Since the NFS version 4 is used, you should add the following entries in the **/etc/default/nfs-common** file:

NEED_IDMAPD=yes
NEED_GSSD=no #no is default

Note: You need to enable GSSD if you are using Kerberos for security, look at the entry **man gssd**.

Step 3

Start the autofs service

$ sudo /etc/init.d/autofs start

The answer should be:

[ok] Starting autofs (via systemctl): autofs.service.

Step 4

Did it work? Let's check the **/new** directory:

sujata@sujata-vm:/new$ ls -l
total 0

There seems to be nothing. This is the magic of autofs, you should explicitly go to share1 or share2 , that is when **autofs** is activated. So only when you access the shared directory, it is only THEN mounted.

$ cd share1
sujata@sujata-vm:/new/share1

```
sujata@sujata-vm:/new$ ls -l
total 8
drwxr-xr-x 2 nobody nogroup 4096 Dec 11 09:20 share1
drwxr-xr-x 2 nobody nogroup 4096 Dec 14 22:48 share2
```

Yes, it does.

Chapter 6 NFS integration with cloud storage

NFS integration with cloud storage

NFS integration with cloud storage has become an essential need for many organizations who want to leverage cloud storage as a part of their infrastructure. Amazon Web Services (AWS) provides a way to integrate NFS with its cloud storage service, Amazon Elastic File System (Amazon EFS). This chapter will provide an overview of NFS integration with Amazon EFS and its benefits.

Amazon EFS

Amazon EFS is a fully managed, elastic, and scalable file storage service designed for use with Amazon EC2 instances. It provides a simple, scalable, and highly available shared file system for use with Linux-based workloads. Amazon EFS is built to be highly scalable and elastic, providing storage capacity that automatically grows and shrinks as needed. It is designed to support thousands of concurrent connections from multiple EC2 instances and can scale to petabyte-level file systems.

NFS Integration with Amazon EFS

Amazon EFS is designed to be accessible from multiple EC2 instances, making it an ideal solution for organizations that need to share files across multiple instances. Amazon EFS supports the Network File System (NFS) protocol, which enables seamless integration with NFS clients running on EC2 instances. This integration allows EC2 instances to mount the Amazon EFS file system as a shared network drive and access files as if they were on a local disk.

To integrate NFS with Amazon EFS, you need to create an Amazon EFS file system, configure the security group settings, and create mount targets in the same VPC as the EC2 instances that will access the file system. You will also need to install NFS client software on the EC2 instances that will access the file system.

Once the NFS client software is installed on the EC2 instances, you can mount the Amazon EFS file system as a network drive using the mount command. The file system can then be accessed by any application running on the EC2 instances as if it were a local disk.

Benefits of NFS Integration with Amazon EFS

Integrating NFS with Amazon EFS provides several benefits, including:

Scalability: Amazon EFS provides scalable storage capacity that automatically grows and shrinks as needed. This enables organizations to easily accommodate changes in workload and storage requirements without having to manually manage storage capacity.

Cost-Effective: Amazon EFS provides a cost-effective solution for organizations that need to share files across multiple instances. It eliminates the need for organizations to invest in expensive storage hardware and infrastructure.

Highly Available: Amazon EFS is designed to be highly available, providing multiple availability zones for data redundancy. This ensures that data is always available, even in the event of a failure.

Simple Management: Amazon EFS is a fully managed service, which means that AWS takes care of all the maintenance and management tasks. This frees up IT resources and allows organizations to focus on their core business objectives.

NFS integration with Amazon EFS is an excellent solution for organizations that need to share files across multiple instances. It provides a cost-effective, scalable, and highly available shared file system that is easy to manage. By leveraging the benefits of Amazon EFS, organizations can improve their infrastructure and simplify their storage management.

Chapter 7 NFS performance tuning

NFS is a widely used protocol for sharing files and directories over a network. However, like any other system, NFS can experience performance issues, especially when dealing with large data sets or high volumes of traffic. Fortunately, there are several techniques available to tune NFS performance and optimize its speed and reliability.

Here are some key NFS performance tuning techniques and examples of the commands used to implement them:

Adjusting buffer sizes: NFS uses several buffers to optimize data transfer between the client and server. The size of these buffers can significantly impact performance, so it's important to adjust them according to your needs. The following commands can be used to adjust the buffer sizes:

Step 1

rsize and wsize: These parameters specify the read and write buffer sizes, respectively. They can be set using the mount command, for example:

mount -t nfs -o rsize=32768,wsize=32768 192.168.1.5:/export /mnt/nfs

In this example, the read and write buffer sizes are set to 32 KB.

tcp_nodelay: This parameter disables the Nagle algorithm, which can improve performance for small packets. It can be set using the mount command as well:

mount -t nfs -o tcp_nodelay 192.168.1.5:/export /mnt/nfs

Enabling this option may lead to higher network utilization and increased CPU usage on both the client and server.

Step 2

Adjusting NFS settings: There are several NFS-specific parameters that can be adjusted to optimize performance. These parameters can be set in the NFS configuration file (/etc/nfs.conf on most systems) or using the sysctl command. Here are some examples:

nfs.nfsdthreads: This parameter controls the number of threads used by the NFS server daemon (nfsd). Increasing the number of threads can improve performance, especially for multi-core systems. The default value is usually 8, but it can be increased to a higher number, for example:

sysctl -w nfs.nfsdthreads=16

nfsd.max_threads: This parameter sets the maximum number of threads that the NFS server daemon can use. It can also be adjusted using the sysctl command, for example:

sysctl -w nfsd.max_threads=64

Note: that increasing the number of threads may require additional system resources, such as CPU and memory.

Step 3

Tuning file system settings: The file system used by NFS can also impact performance. Here are some examples of file system tuning commands:

noatime: This option disables the update of access times on files, which can reduce disk I/O and improve performance. It can be set in the mount options, for example:

mount -t nfs -o noatime 192.168.1.5:/export /mnt/nfs

sync: This option forces NFS to write data to the server immediately, rather than buffering it. This can improve data integrity but may impact performance. It can also be set in the mount options, for example:

mount -t nfs -o sync 192.168.1.5:/export /mnt/nfs

Note that enabling this option may lead to higher network utilization and increased CPU usage on both the client and server.

By implementing these NFS performance tuning techniques, you can optimize the speed and reliability of your NFS file sharing system. However, it's important to carefully monitor the system and adjust the settings as needed to ensure optimal performance.

Chapter 8 Network File System version 4

NFSv4, or Network File System version 4, is the fourth iteration of the popular distributed file system protocol, originally developed by Sun Microsystems. NFSv4 offers a number of new features and improvements over its predecessor, NFSv3. In this chapter, we will delve deep into the features and benefits of NFSv4, exploring the ways in which it can improve the performance, security, and reliability of distributed file systems.

NFSv4 was first introduced in 2000, with the publication of RFC 3530. It represented a significant departure from the previous version of NFS, NFSv3, which had been in use since the late 1990s. NFSv4 was designed to address a number of shortcomings in NFSv3, including performance bottlenecks, security vulnerabilities, and limited support for modern network technologies. The result was a protocol that was more scalable, more secure, and more flexible than its predecessor.

One of the key features of NFSv4 is its support for stateful operations. In NFSv3, each file operation was stateless, meaning that the client had to explicitly request each operation from the server. In NFSv4, however, the server maintains a stateful session with the client, allowing for more efficient file operations. This stateful architecture also enables features such as file locking, which was not possible in NFSv3.

Another significant feature of NFSv4 is its support for strong authentication and encryption. NFSv4 introduces a new security model, known as NFSv4 Security, which provides enhanced security features such as Kerberos authentication, integrity checking, and encryption. This makes NFSv4 much more secure than NFSv3, which had limited support for authentication and no support for encryption.

NFSv4 also includes a number of performance optimizations. For example, it supports larger block sizes for file transfers, allowing for faster data transfer rates over high-speed networks. It also includes support for parallel I/O operations, which can improve performance on multi-core systems. NFSv4 also introduces new caching mechanisms, which can reduce the amount of data that needs to be transferred over the network.

One of the most notable improvements in NFSv4 is its support for file delegations. File delegations allow a client to temporarily assume exclusive access to a file, which can improve performance and reduce network traffic. For example, if a client is performing a sequence of operations on a file, NFSv4 can delegate the file to the client, allowing it to perform the operations locally without needing to send requests to the server for each operation.

NFSv4 also includes support for server-side copy operations. Server-side copying allows the server to perform file operations locally, without needing to send data back and forth over the network. This can significantly improve performance on high-latency networks, such as those found in cloud environments.

In addition to these core features, NFSv4 includes a number of other improvements over NFSv3. For example, it introduces support for file attributes, which allows clients to retrieve information about files such as creation date, modification date, and file size. It also includes improved support for ACLs (Access Control Lists), which can provide finer-grained control over file permissions.

Despite these many improvements, NFSv4 has not been widely adopted in production environments. This is largely due to the complexity of implementing the protocol, as well as the fact that many legacy systems still rely on NFSv3. However, with the continued growth of cloud computing and distributed storage systems, NFSv4 may become more relevant in the coming years.

In conclusion, NFSv4 represents a significant step forward in the evolution of distributed file systems. Its stateful architecture, strong security features, and performance optimizations make it a powerful tool for managing distributed storage.

www.ingramcontent.com/pod-product-compliance
Lightning Source LLC
Chambersburg PA
CBHW080545060326
40690CB00022B/5225

* 9 7 9 8 3 8 6 7 4 0 2 0 7 *